KATY PERRY
WITNESS

PIANO
VOCAL
GUITAR

T0086645

ISBN 978-1-5400-0103-0

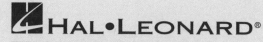

HAL•LEONARD®

7777 W. BLUEMOUND RD. P.O. BOX 13819 MILWAUKEE, WI 53213

In Australia Contact:
Hal Leonard Australia Pty. Ltd.
4 Lentara Court
Cheltenham, Victoria, 3192 Australia
Email: ausadmin@halleonard.com.au

WITNESS

Words and Music by KATY PERRY,
MAX MARTIN, SAVAN KOTECHA
and ALI PAYAMI

this.

Amaj7

(Will you be my wit-ness?

F#m7

Could you be the one who speaks for me?

C#m7

N.C.   **D.S. al Coda**

We're all just

CODA

this. Oh.   (Ah.)

Amaj7   N.C.

HEY HEY HEY

Words and Music by KATY PERRY,
MAX MARTIN, SIA FURLER,
ALI PAYAMI and SARAH HUDSON

*Lead vocal written an octave higher.

ROULETTE

Words and Music by KATY PERRY,
MAX MARTIN, SHELLBACK,
ALI PAYAMI and FERRAS ALQAISI

I'm up-tight, ___ play-ing by the rules in this game ___ of life. ___ Three hun-dred six-ty five days on ___ the grind. ___ Some-thing's stir-ring, I might need to ___ un-wind. ___ Then,

SWISH SWISH

Words and Music by KATY PERRY,
DUKE DUMONT, SARAH HUDSON,
ONIKA MARAJ, PJ SLEDGE,
BRITTANY HAZZARD and ROLAND CLARK

Moderately fast

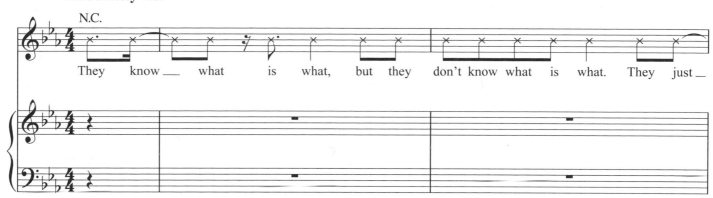

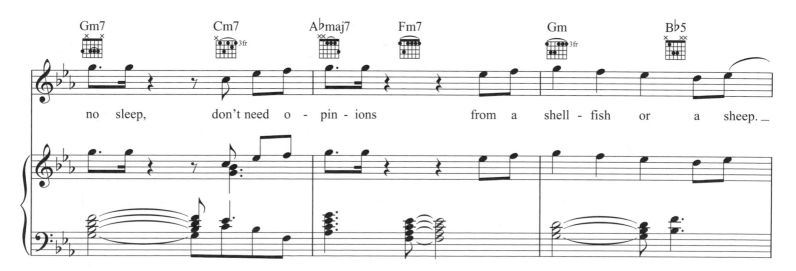

* Vocal written an octave higher than sung.

Additional Lyrics

Rap I: Pink Ferragamo sliders on deck.
Silly rap beefs just get me more checks.
My life is a movie; I'm never off set.
Me and my a-MIGOS, (no, not OFFSET.)

Swish, swish, ah, I got them upset,
But my shooters'll make 'em dance like dub step.
Swish, swish, aww, my haters is obsessed,
'Cause I make Ms, they get MUCH LESS.

Rap II: Damn, man, this bitch is a Stan.
Muah, muah, the generous queen will kiss a fan.
Ass, goodbye, I'm-a be riding by.
I'm-a tell my biggz, "Yeah, dat's da guy."

A star's a star. Da-ha, da-ha.
They never thought the swish God would take it this far.
Get my pimp cup, this is pimp shit, baby.
I only fuck with Queens, so I'm making hits with Katy.

DÉJÀ VU

Words and Music by KATY PERRY,
HAYDEN LUBY, FERRAS ALQAISI
and THOMAS STELL

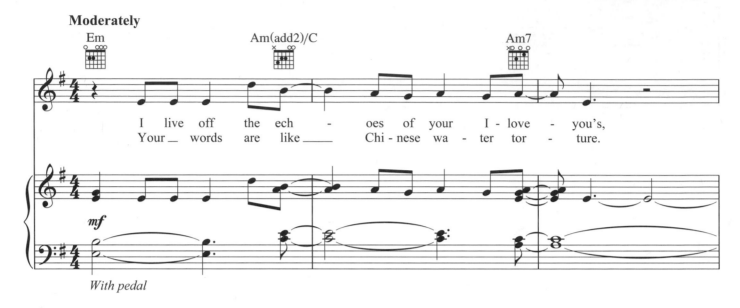

I live off the ech - oes of your I - love - you's,
Your __ words are like _____ Chi - nese wa - ter tor - ture.

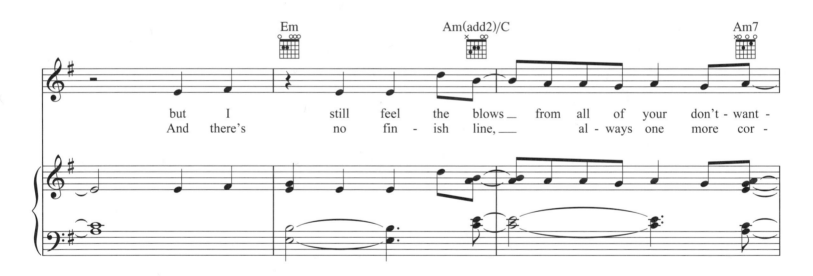

but I still feel the blows __ from all of your don't - want -
And there's no fin - ish line, ___ al - ways one more cor -

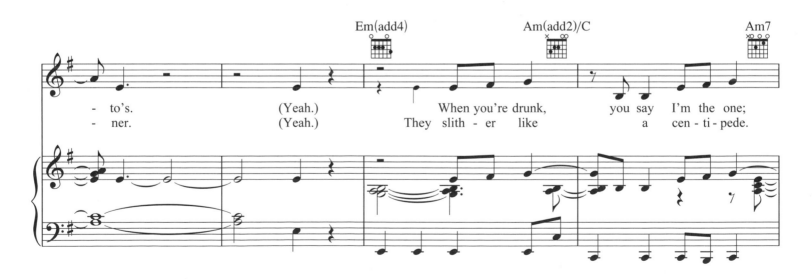

- to's. (Yeah.) When you're drunk, you say I'm the one;
- ner. (Yeah.) They slith - er like a cen - ti - pede.

Solo ends   'Cause

ev - 'ry day's the same, _____   def - i - ni - tion of in - sane.   I think we're

run - ning on a loop; _____   dé - jà vu.   (Dé - jà vu,   dé - jà vu,

POWER

Words and Music by KATY PERRY,
JACK GARRATT and SMOKEY ROBINSON

Pop Ballad

mp

drum fill

I was fine be - fore __ I met __ you. Truth is __ __ that I lost my - self __ in - side __ you. It is __

To Coda

ing my pow - er, pow - er.

MIND MAZE

Words and Music by KATY PERRY,
SARAH HUDSON, CORIN RODDICK
and MEGAN JAMES

Moderately slow, in 2

I'm los-ing all __ di-rec - tion, slip-ping in - to quick - sand. I've shat-tered the __ il-lu - sion seen be-hind __ the cur - tain. __

sub - mit to the sweet _____ sur - ren - der?

It's a

MISS YOU MORE

Words and Music by KATY PERRY,
SARAH HUDSON, CORIN RODDICK
and MEGAN JAMES

To Coda

D.S. al Coda

We were a match, but not a fit. _____ We were a

dream, un-re-al-is-tic. We did-n't lose, we did-n't win. ___

___ (Some-times I won-der what we could have been.) I miss you

CHAINED TO THE RHYTHM

Words and Music by KATY PERRY,
MAX MARTIN, SIA FURLER,
ALI PAYAMI and SKIP MARLEY

Moderate Dance Pop

Are we cra - zy? Liv-ing our lives through a lens. Trapped in our white pick - et fence like or -

TSUNAMI

Words and Music by KATY PERRY,
MICHAEL WILLIAMS, MARCUS BELL,
SARAH HUDSON and MIA MORETTI

Moderate Pop Ballad

Please don't tip - toe, come close, let's flow.
Don't fight, just ride the rhy - thm of the tide.

An - chor in me, and get lost at sea.
We swirl, in we spin, salt - ed, sun - kissed skin

The world's your oys - ter and I am the pearl.
We float to - geth - er, what - ev - er weath - er.

BON APPETIT

Words and Music by KATY PERRY,
MAX MARTIN, SHELLBACK,
OSCAR HOLTER, FERRAS ALQAISI,
QUAVIOUS MARSHALL, KIARI CEPHUS
and KIRSNICK BALL

Moderate Dance groove

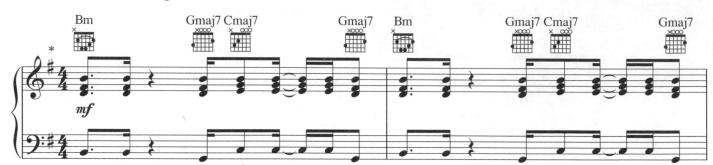

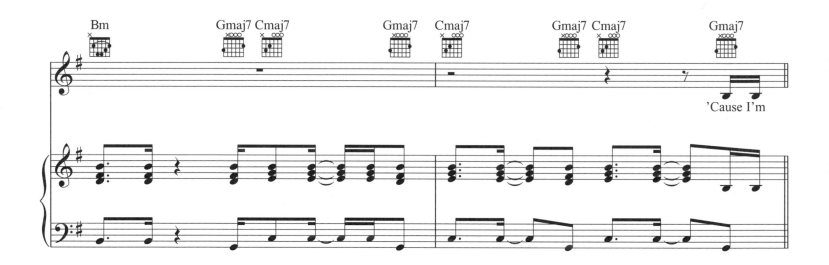

'Cause I'm

all that you want, boy, ___ all that you can have, boy. ___ Got me

* Recorded a half step lower.

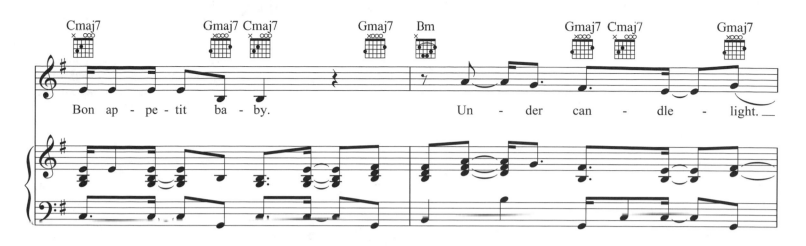

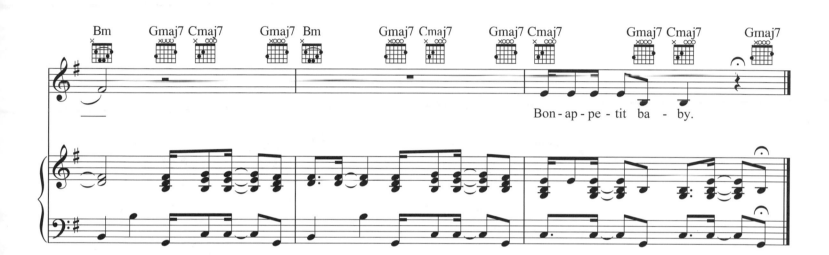

Additional Lyrics

Rap: I'm the one they say can change your life.
No waterfall, she drippin' wet, you like my ice? (blast)
She say she want a Migo night. Now I ask her, "What the price?" (hold on)
If she do right, told her get whatever you like.
I grab her legs and now divide, aight.
Make her do a donut when she ride, aight.
Looking at the eyes of a dime make you blind.
In her spine, and my diamonds change the climate.
Sweet tooth, no tooth fairy.
Whipped cream, no dairy.
Got her hot light on screaming, "I'm ready."
But no horses, no carriage.

BIGGER THAN ME

Words and Music by KATY PERRY,
SARAH HUDSON, CORIN RODDICK
and MEGAN JAMES

SAVE AS DRAFT

Words and Music by KATY PERRY,
NOONIE BAO, DIJON McFARLANE,
NICHOLAS AUDINO, LEWIS HUGHES
and ELOF LOELV

PENDULUM

Words and Music by KATY PERRY,
JEFF BHASKER and SARAH HUDSON

Moderate Pop beat

You got pa-ti-na, ain't so green, ____ no. ___ You earned this spot, got your re-ceipts, ____ yeah. _ Fun-ny, got-ta add ad-den-dums to your dreams. ___

D.S. al Coda

just let go.

CODA

all comes back,_ it all comes back a - round._

_____ There is no need_ to wor - ry: the pag - es keep_

_____ on turn - ing, and it goes on and on, comes all the way_ a - round. __

_____ There is no need_ to hur - ry: if there's a fi -

INTO ME YOU SEE

Words and Music by KATY PERRY,
ALEXIS TAYLOR, JOE GODDARD
and FERRAS ALQAISI